# Submissions

*A 31 day devotional of Reflections, Praises in Poetry From an Islamic Perspective*

Published by
UniqueVerses Publishing
Charlotte, N. C.

Submissions
By Fareed Abdus-Saboor Hood (Rickey K. Hood)
Copyright © 1995
Registered with the Library of Congress
All rights reserved. No reproduction,
Copy or reprinting of this book is permitted
Accept by the author's permission.

Published by UniqueVerses Publishing
In Charlotte, N. C.

ISBN # 0-9678457-3-4

With Gratitude

Giving all Praises and thanks to Allah (God), the Lord of the Worlds, for all He has done for me and giving thanks to my Mother, Effie L. Hood, who taught me to look into myself and bring out the good always. Thanks to my brother Ronnie and my niece Katischa for being the wall I bounce my poems off of.

Table of Contents:

*Reflections:*

# Reflections

# 1
## Trust

*"Verily! Allah commands that you should render back the trust to those to whom they are due..." Surah 4:58.*

No trust no faith. Imagine yourself standing on top of a bench with arms folded and your eyes shut. A group of people standing behind you urging you to fall backward and that they'll catch you. The feeling of anxiety starts to surge through your stomach; your heart begins pumping fast and sweat spring off your face in little-wet balls. A voice in your head is telling you to trust them; another voice is saying "forget it! No way." Like a fork in a road, you find yourself being split in half, but you can only choose one way to go. A decision must be made; trust or no trust? Begin with trust. Without trust, you will fail. Where there is no trust one will find the effects of doubt, suspicion, uncertainty, mistrust. If you submit yourself to God as a Muslim then you must trust Allah. You must trust him through the difficulties in life, and the good times in life. You must trust Allah in all areas of life, good and bad. Allah will guide you, comfort you and protect you when you trust him in all things.

Think to yourself in times of decision, "I will trust God and I will fall backward into His strong loving arms." Trust.

## 2
## *Fearful*

*"...but when the fighting was ordained for them, behold! A section of them fears men as they fear Allah or even more." Surah 4:77.*

To be fearful of those who have power over you is a natural part of living. We see in men the strength they possess, the harm and good they can cause. We look to their strength as our blessing or harm and forget about the Lord of the Worlds. Fear of men is an enemy to man. Fear is a wall that will stop you. Fear will stop you from doing the good you ought to do, or fulfilling the dreams you desire. The only way over the wall is to have faith in God and remember He is the Power, He gives blessing and harm; none can resist Him. Trust Allah and make no excuses. Fall back into His loving arms and let God's word (the Qur'an) and his Messenger (Muhammad, peace be upon him) guide your life. Open your heart to your brother, trust in God, Trust in Islam and don't be afraid to love one another.

Think and reflect: "Is there a wall I need to get over today?"

## 3
## Order

*"Do people think that they will be left alone*
*Because they say: "we have faith" and will not*
*be tested." Surah 29: 2*


Nothing worth having has ever been easily gotten. It hurts to go against our lower nature to do what is right and orderly. To pray, fast and submit are obligations on people of faith, on the contrary, to believe that God will accept disobedience is to believe that God will accept anything. Be thankful the Allah has put an order in our lives. Walking in the truth is not an easy thing to do but the rewards for believing God and faithfully obeying Him out weight the hardships and weakness you have now.
  Trust Allah.

## 4
### Faith

*"The Lord of the heavens and earth and all
that is between them, if you (but) have faith
with certainty." Surah 44:7.*

Faith is like the sun; there are days when one wakes up
with faith brightly shining, a perfect day when nothing will
seem to go wrong, but slowly and quietly clouds of life's
realities begins rolling in and weaken the bright intensity
of faith. The day becomes gloomy, dim and the light
slowly fades. Later the wind and rain of hardships begin
to pour down. Where then is the faith you begin with?
Have the uncertainties of life taken it away? No, faith is
there if you believe in Allah, bright and shining as ever.
Faith is above the clouds, above the hardships above the
storm as it rages. It rest and resides securely in the abode
of the knowledge of God and His love for us. Faith shines
knowing that Allah is always there.

## 5
### Patience

*Abu de Darda reported that Allah's Messenger*
*(Peace be upon him) said, "On the day of resurrection,*
*nothing will weigh better in the Scales of any of Allah's*
*slaves then good character. Truly Allah detests the wicked*
*and foul tongues."*
*Jewels of Guidance, Chapter 15.*

One problem in the Ummah (Community) is Muslim impatience with Muslim. Fault finding is a daily affair and acknowledging good in each other has become rare. Most Muslims do not have enough patience to find the good in their brothers. Hence, the effects produce by impatience are gossip, slander, discord, and mistrust. Some may think that they are God fearing people and above the people they criticize. Others may believe they are blameless and justified in their criticism, but Allah knows every man's heart, what is revealed or concealed.

Think and reflect, ask yourself if you're guilty of pointing a finger at another's faults while you yourself are neck deep in your own wrongs. Repent daily before Allah, the Most Merciful, and do good. Start the work of patience in your life and restrain your tongue. Be mindful of your brother.

## 6
### Good

*Narrated anas: The Prophet (peace be upon him) said, "None of you will have faith till he likes for his brother what he likes for himself. Summarized Sahih Al-Bukhari, page 61.*

Good is what everyone wants but not what everyone wants to be. Some believers are selfish and lacking in compassion. They are driven by monetary success and not the success of doing what is good and right. Think of what is being sacrificed in the pursuit of things. Is love for your fellow Muslims lacking? The act of loving is a human choice and a Godly command; it is not based solely on emotion but rather obedience; obedience to Allah and His Messenger. Think how you can today seek to improve yourself to the glory of God as well as improve the lives of those around you. The choice to love, to express concern for our fellow man is not an easy thing to do. It takes time, patience and hard work but the effort will be worth it.

In conclusion, pray for others, focus on others, have a loving heart for others, hope for others, have faith in others and do it all in love. This is good.

# 7
## *Successful*

"And whosoever is saved from his covetousness,
such are they who will be successful." Surah 59:9.

Who do you consider successful? Choose from your
mental list of successful people. Are the loving parents
who raised you on that list? Are the persons who had little
yet had enough to share with you on that list? Are those
who risked and gave their lives for our rights and
privileges, which we take for granted, on that mental list of
successful people? Make it your intention to take care of
the needs of others and stop focusing on self. If you are
strong in faith help those who are weak. If you are
wealthy in knowledge, enrich those who are poor. If you
have material wealth, help those who are in need. Be open
and humble yourself to the needs of others. "Such are they
who will be successful"

*8*
*One Ummah*

*On the authority of Abu Huraira, who said:*
*"The Messenger of Allah (Peace be upon him) said,*
*'Do not envy one another; do not inflate prices one to*
*another; do not hate one another; do not turn away from*
*one another and do not undercut one another, but be you,*
*O servants of Allah, brothers.'"*
*Forty Hadith #38.*

Respect for one another is essential in Islam if brotherhood is to be maintained. Faith is determined by deeds and behavior; likewise, deeds and behavior can influence faith for the better or worse in others. When brothers meet it should be for the love of Allah, not the contrary of thinking to have an advantage over another brother in wealth or knowledge so to believe you're better than he; this is not an act of love but enmity. Brothers should be aware of the levels of faith in one another and do nothing to weaken that faith. If one cannot be an example of good, then don't seek to be an example of bad. Brotherhood is conditional on respect and trust. If brotherhood is polluted with mistrust and bad deeds then it cannot function. Any good that is done for the sake of Allah should not be considered the sole benefit of any one person or group, but for the benefit of the whole community. In contrast, any bad deed that is done by a Muslim becomes the public image of every Muslim. Be very careful and conscious of how you present yourself to others.

Respect one another for the sake of Islam and don't become sidetracked by differences of opinion. Only in true brotherhood: love, respect, and patience can we grow to become One Ummah.

## 9
### *Sincerity*

*"And obey Allah and the Messenger that
you may obtain mercy" Surah 3:132.*


A brother may say that he loves Allah but does he reflect that sincerity in his life?  "Peace be upon you" and "If it is Allah's will" are part of his daily speech, but how often does he peacefully gives charity to those in need and how much of God's will does he put into practice?  "Deeds are by intention..." (Forty Hadith #1) the Prophet (peace be upon him) said, hence, good intentions should produce good deeds. Think to yourself and ask, "I'm I sincere, do my intentions produce good deeds?"

Avoid useless talk, and focus on sincerity.  Love for Allah is not based on feelings alone, but sincerity and obedience.

## 10
## Shooting Star

*Narrated by Abu Sa'id Al-khudri: Allah's Messenger (peace be upon him) said, "If a person embraces Islam sincerely, then Allah shall forgive all his past sins…"*
*Summarized Sahih Al-Bukhari, page 71.*

How many people have you known that live their lives like shooting stars? They having bright beautiful promising beginnings find themselves burned out due to their lack of sincerity; many live their spiritual lives in just the same way. Enthusiastically they believe in the message they hear, then join the place of worship to later realize the spiritual commitment involved turn away hearing of some other faith movement and flee to be part of that flock. Rarely do they stay with a teacher long enough to mature to a fundamental understanding of their faith. They are like shooting stars flying all over the spiritual sky seeking instant knowledge, quick recognition, microwaves results without supplying the required time, dedication, and self-sacrifice necessary to obtain the desired end result.

Don't be a shooting star. Stand still; focus yourself on your religious education. Be a servant to Allah raised up and shining like one of his bright stars.

## 11
### Perfection

*Thy Guardian –Lord hath not forsaken thee,*
*nor is the he displeased.  Surah 93:3.*


You may think at times that you have done something wrong and that God has rejected you and may begin to feel helpless and depressed.  The human attribute of making mistakes often weaken spiritual esteem.  Thus, the worship of Allah may become acts of ritual rather than acts of reverence.  In this state of being (or spirit), you may wrongfully perceive God to be dogmatic, demanding that his servants be perfectionist in righteousness.  This is not true, perfection is with Allah only not in mankind.  Allah does not seek perfection in his servants but faith and sincerity.

In times of weakness seek help from The Most Gracious and forgiveness from The Most Merciful.  Seek refuge in The Oft-Returning and rest in The Most Forbearing, confidently with striving worship none but Allah.  This is the closest we can get to perfection.

## 12
### Peer Pressure

*"O Uncle! By God almighty I swear, even if
they should put the sun in my right hand and the
moon in my left that I adjure this cause, I shall  not do so
until God had vindicated it or cause me to perish in the
process." The Life of Muhammad, page 89.*


Sometimes you may feel inadequate or out of place because of the decision to be a servant of Allah.  However, you must determine whether you really feel that way or are you feeling the negativity of those around you. Seeking to please God and not a man will not make you popular, for example: wearing modest clothing, making time for prayer, not participating in none Muslim holidays can make you stand out as different.  At times, you may even become singled out for bigoted reasons and get very frightened and feel very alone. It can be a price we pay when seeking the straight path.

Don't let peer pressure be a ruling force in your life, even if you are offered the sun and moon.  Trust God and He will restore your peace of mind and spirit.

## 13
### Advisors

*"And he (Satan) swore to them both*
*(Adam and Eve) that he was their sincere adviser"*

The life of man is as a budding flower. In the bloom of his life he is beautiful and young, experiencing the joys of living with all the foolishness he desire; living seamlessly immortal days of youth until time touches him, and he notices that he is growing old. If it is God's will, his knowledge and experiences will develop into maturity that will in time grow to become wisdom. He will become like those before him, a storehouse of knowledge and experiences for those seeking truth and understanding.

The life of a man is as a withering flower. Once being beautiful and young, he now stands gray and bent. Pray that Allah grants you guidance as you travel through life's journey. Seek to become wise and not a foolish old man. Seek advice from those whom Allah has made wise and be ever mindful that age does not equal maturity. Choose your advisors carefully.

## 14
## Read!

*"Read! In the name of your Lord who has created…
Read! And your Lord is the Most Generous, who
has taught by the pen; has taught man that which
he did not know" Surah 96:1-5.*

"Feed me, feed me," that is the attitude that some have in learning their religion. They prefer to sit and to take what is given to them by the speaker while seldom studying for themselves to obtain a better understanding of what they are being taught. They are spiritual toddlers who are not qualified to teach others, and some of these seek positions of leadership and some are in such positions. They feed their communities the knowledge they have gleaned from types or videos etc. without checking the source the information is coming from to know if they were taught correctly. The blind leading the blind.

Grab onto the lifeline that Allah has given us. It is the responsibility of each Muslim to know his religion for his and herself and not accept blindly what is given. The Prophet (peace be upon him) said that he has left us two things, the Qur'an and his Sunnah (Hadith). Study, read and understand to qualify yourself before Allah as maturing.

## 15
### Whirlwinds

*Have We not lifted up your heart and*
*relieved you of your burden, which weighed down your*
*back? Surah 94:1-4.*

Like ships blown off course, the whirlwind of life's confusions has sent many of us into disarray. We fight and struggle against what seem to be impossible odds and feel that no one understands what we're going through or that no one else has gone through such an ordeal as ours. In truth, many will understand because they have gone through the same storms and found their way back on course. Remember the boycott, when many Muslims suffered and died for Islam; the Prophet (peace be upon him) strengthen them to have patience and trust in Allah. Allah Most High has promised us toil and hardships in this life. There is nothing that can be done to avoid it, but we can be made stronger in the hardships if we seek refuge in Him. He has promised relief if we endure the hardships, "So verily, with hardship there is a relief, verily with the hardship there is a relief." Surah 94:5-6.

Seek refuge in Allah and take pleasure in His name, Al-Wadud "The Loving One." Find the peaceful course that is straight and maintain it for the pleasure of Allah.

# 16
## Uniqueness

"And if your Lord had so willed, He could surely have made mankind one community, but he will not cease to disagree." Surah 11:18.

Individuality, being different and expressing one's self are parts of this beautiful world God has made of us. It is a blessing to be different and a blessing to come together in union. True unity does not come by becoming what people impose on you, but rather what you choose for yourself for the love of Allah and the community. There will never be a total agreement of opinion in any group of people, but this is the price we pay for uniqueness among God's creation. Good relationships between believing people are not easy but something that is necessary. Accepting differences and uniting as a community is a challenge given to us by Allah. We must meet the challenge and the blessing of free-will that make us above the beast, or our animal nature will make us savages tearing the Ummah apart. Love your brothers and come together in Islam.

Think to yourself, "am I letting petty differences keep me away from my brothers."

## 17
### Let's make a deal

*"Truly, those who believe and do righteous good works, for them will be an endless reward that will never stop (i.e. Paradise)." Surah 41:8*

Most people come to faith in God with a bargaining mentality. They think that if they give their lives to God that He owes them something in return. The belief that if I become a God loving person everything in my life will be smoother, God will make a way through all my problems and everything in my life will be made blessed and easy. But a blessed life never comes easily. God has never inspired a "let's make a deal" religion, I give Him faith and He gives me what I want. No, it is about committing yourself to the Lord of the Universe and acknowledging Allah as your Lord. Being aware that if you worship Allah as your God or not Allah is still God and we are His slaves. Can a slave bargain with his master? Investing faith in God only to expect a miracle in return is selfish and unrealistic.

Allah has not promised us miracles as a prize for believing in him (though He is more than able) but He has promised that our faith will be rewarded in this life, as He sees fit to reward it, and in the Here-After.

*Ambition*

*"Those who believe and migrated [by faith to Islam]
and strove hard and fought in Allah's cause with their
wealth and their lives are far higher in degree in Allah's
sight. They are successful." Surah 9:20*

You only get that watch you strive for in this life. Striving is a test of endurance to fulfill an ambition; if the ambition is to achieve monetary or some other mundane fortune, then you will eventually attain your goal. Think and reflect on what this worldly striving has achieved, nothing but things that will wear out and get thrown away or passed to another after your death. What have you really gained from your work if your ambition is for earthly gain? On the other hand, if your ambition is to worship Allah, then He will permit you the wealth of this world and the Paradise of the Hereafter. What is your ambition?

## Atonement

*Pray, "Our Lord! Condemn us not if we*
*forget or fall into error... Blot our sin,*
*and grant us forgiveness." Surah 2:286.*

To seek atonement of wrongdoing is an innate desire for those seeking to do right. No one can continue to live a life of rebellion against their own conscious while at the same time hoping to live a life of faith. Recognizing the necessity for reconciliation with our Creator is challenging and painful. It takes major responsibility, maturity and determination to see a deviation from the path of doing what is right and take the essential steps to correct the departure. Allah has said that he will make easy the path we follow. If it is the path to Allah He will make it easy. Allah is the Most Gracious and Merciful and He will accept all who turn to Him for forgiveness and will turn no one away. Allah is most merciful.

# Praises
# In
# Poetry

## 20
## Praises

*I will praise the Lord and be not ashamed*
*I will praise Him when I am alone*
*I will praise Him before the world*

*Praise Him without faltering my spirit*
*Praise Him with truth on my tongue*
*Praise Him in the early dawn*
*Praise Him when the moon shines its light*
*Praise Him*

## 21
### The Wise

*How beautiful, how beautiful is Al-Hakim,*
*the Perfectly Wise*
*Awake all you sleepers of knowledge*
*And see the Lord's wisdom*
*For with it He created the worlds.*

*Know not the Lord's love for us?*
*Awake with understanding*
*See the beauty of creation*
*Founded by Allah's wisdom.*

*22*
*A Poem of Praise*

*Praise be the day*
*Of might and man*
*Of tears and sorrows*
*Of joys overflowing*

*Praise the day*
*All humbled hands and bowing eyes*
*Of arms raised in mighty prayers*

*Let him be praised*
*Through temptation and frustrations*
*Setbacks and despairs*

*Praise be the day*
*When thoughts of giving up*
*Fade to night*
*And renewed strength rises with the morn*

*Praise be/ Praise him*
*Praise be to God in all things*
*Great and small/ blessings and hardships*
*Triumphs and defeats/ heartbreaks and new loves*
*And all that come*
*With a life well lived*

## 23
### All I have

*All that I have*
*I offer to you*
*My little bowl of thanks*
*Full and ripe with gratitude/ tears*
*Years of joy/ sorrows*
*All that I am*
*I give you*
*Patience/ caring/ hopes*
*My bowl is full*
*Take it*
*This is all I have*

## 24
### Hope

*In the midst of my misfortune*
*I found a chest of gold*
*Full of dreams/ faith/ and hopes*
*A comfort since days of old*

*In the midst of my misfortune*
*I found a golden light*
*Shining deeply in my soul*
*Guiding me through this night*

*In the midst of my misfortune*
*In the depth of my despair*
*I raised my eyes toward the heavens*
*And found you standing there*

*A treasure/ in the midst of my misfortune*

*25*
*Miracles*

*Miracle: sweet angelic wings*
*Brushing against mundane lives*
*Giving life*

*Miracle: the hand of the Loving One*
*Reaching through hardships*
*And temptations*
*Giving hope*

*Miracle of miracles: a life raised*
*From death/ full of expectation*
*A hope/ full of expectation*
*Giving praise*

*26*
*Step one:*

*Love thyself*
*Know thyself*
*Be thyself*
*Forgive thyself*
*Seek thyself*
*Find thyself*
*Battle thyself*
*Comfort thyself*
*Make peace with thyself*
*Bring out the God in thyself*

*Step two:*
*Love others/ as thyself*

# 27
## He is God

God is not some abstract
Feeling/ thought/ or belief
I don't think myself so naive
He is real
Real/ as the air I breathe
Real/ as the earth that supports me

I have seen God
Not with eyes/ they deceive
The God I know
Is seen by faith
Seen in His scriptures
Seen in His creation
Seen in His people

My God is The Eternal/ Ever Present/ Real
"I am not a man that I should lie,
Nor a son of man that I should change my mind" (1)
"Say, He is God, the One...
He does not give birth, nor has He ever been born..."(2)

No religion can own Him
His truth is for all people

"Hear, O Israel, the Lord your God is One"(3)
"Say not Trinity, for your Guardian Lord is One"(4)
The Eternal is God
Nothing that came afterwards is He

He is before the beginning
And shall be after the end
He is before the Alpha
And after the Omega

He is God

(1)   Numbers 23:19, (2) Surah 112, (3) Deut.6:4, (4)Surah 4:171

*28*
*Life Time*

*Pressures of existing*
*Has shaped me in many forms*
*Many styles*
*As long as I live*
*It shall continue to shape me*

*My final form*
*I do not know/ nor does it matter*
*In one life time I've lived many lives*

*My final form?*
*What does it matter?*
*So long that I have lived*

*29*
*Peace is…*

*Peace is…*
*A soft breeze brushing against the soul*
*a friend holding my hand*

*Peace is…*
*A word of faith*
*a prayer to The Loving One*

*Peace is…*
*A quite place of perfume and beauty*
*A God who care and loves me.*

## 30
### Be Still

*A quite whisper echoes through my soul*
*"Be still"*
*"Be still"*

*Turbulent raging images recede*
*Calm thoughts have become mine again*
*"Be still"*

*My Lord has lead me to find in myself*
*"Peace, be still"*

## 31
### Be true

*How precious*
*It is for a man to be himself*
*For what does it profit God*
*To have a white washed wall.*

*About the Author*

*Fareed Abdus-Saboor Hood received his Bachelors of Arts degree in Religious Studies at The University of North Carolina at Charlotte in 2004 and his Associates in Arts Degree from Central Piedmont Community College in 2002, he also studied at the Islamic Online University where he received several Certifications in Islamic studies.*

www.ingramcontent.com/pod-product-compliance
Lightning Source LLC
Chambersburg PA
CBHW071800020426
42331CB00008B/2337